No AR

S0-AHG-106

Everything You Need to Know About

AN
ALCOHOLIC
PARENT

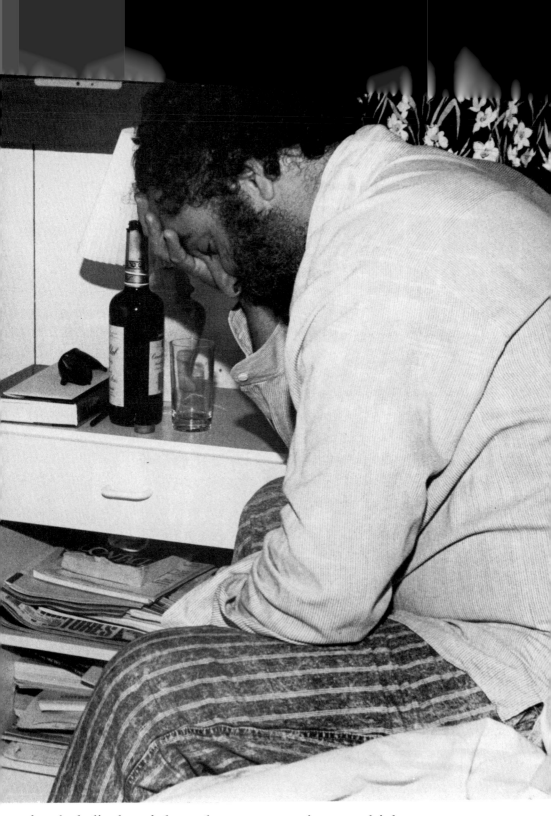

An alcoholic doesn't know how to stop at just one drink.

Everything You Need to Know About

AN ALCOHOLIC PARENT

Nancy Shuker

Series Editor: Evan Stark, Ph.D.

THE ROSEN PUBLISHING GROUP, INC.
NEW YORK

Published in 1990, 1993, 1995, 1998 by The Rosen Publishing Group, Inc.
29 East 21st Street, New York, NY 10010

Revised Edition 1998

Copyright © 1990, 1993, 1995, 1998 by The Rosen Publishing Group, Inc.

All rights reserved. No part of this book may be reproduced in any form without permission in writing from the publisher, except by a reviewer.

PRAIRIE CREEK LIBRARY DISTRICT
Dwight. Illinois

Library of Congress Cataloging-in-Publication Data

Shuker, Nancy.
    Everything you need to know about an alcoholic parent.
        (The Need to know library)
    Includes bibliographical references and index.
    Summary: Offers advice on how to deal with an alcoholic and where to go
for help.
    ISBN 0-8239-2869-1
    1. Alcoholism—Juvenile literature. 2. Children of Alcoholics—Juvenile
literature. [1. Alcoholism. 2. Alcoholics.] I. Title. II. Series.
HV5066.S49 1989
362.29'23—
                                                                89-10703
                                                                CIP
                                                                AC

Manufactured in the United States of America

Contents

Introduction 6

1. What Is Alcoholism? 9

2. Warning Signs of Alcoholism 15

3. A Family Disease 21

4. Reaching Out for Help 29

5. Coping with Emergencies 35

6. What You Can Do for Yourself 41

7. Who Can Help Your Alcoholic Parent? 47

8. Looking at the Future 53

   Glossary 58

   Where to Go for Help 60

   For Further Reading 62

   Index 63

Introduction

Many people enjoy alcohol occasionally. After a long day at work, some parents may like to share a few beers, glasses of wine, or cocktails. Others might drink alcohol to celebrate a special event, such as a birthday, anniversary, or other holiday. There is nothing wrong with drinking alcohol if a person uses it responsibly and in moderation. But some people, called alcoholics, don't just enjoy alcohol: they need it to function in their daily lives.

Alcohol is a drug, and alcoholism is a disease. Alcoholics are people who are addicted to alcohol and who constantly crave it. If you have a parent who is an alcoholic, life can be very difficult. You may feel isolated from your friends and embarrassed by your parent. Many of your friends and classmates may be experiencing similar problems. It is estimated that 6.6 million children and teens under the age of 18 live in a home with at least one alcoholic parent.

Learning about alcoholism is the first step toward understanding it. And understanding alcoholism is the first step toward effectively coping with it. There are things you can do to make your life easier. You may even be able to help your alcoholic parent find help.

If abused, alcohol can be a dangerous, harmful drug.

Having an alcoholic parent affects every member of a family. You can learn to examine the way that alcohol changes relationships within your family. Then you can work on improving those relationships. Remember, you still can care about and love your alcoholic parent. However, you can also learn to love yourself.

Coping with an alcoholic parent means not feeling afraid, ashamed, or guilty. It also means not taking on extra responsibilities to cover up for your parent. By coping with an alcoholic parent you still may be able to live your life fully. You can still make healthy, positive choices for yourself. Your parent's alcoholism does not have to determine your future.

Many people enjoy one or two alcoholic drinks with their meals.

Chapter 1

What Is Alcoholism?

Experts agree that alcoholism is a disease. An alcoholic is not a bad person; he or she is sick. However, no one is completely certain why some people become alcoholics and others don't. Most likely, alcoholism is caused by a complex mix of hereditary (passed through genes from a parent to a child) and environmental factors.

Alcohol Addiction

There are two types of addiction: physical and psychological. Alcohol causes both types. A physical addiction is when a person's body needs alcohol and cannot function normally without it. An alcoholic may show symptoms of withdrawal when he cannot drink. He may shake, sweat, and become irritable.

In the case of a psychological addiction, an alcoholic does not believe that she can live without alcohol. She experiences a compulsive need to drink. Sometimes this craving occurs because she wants to feel alcohol's pleasurable effects. In other cases she is afraid of suffering uncomfortable withdrawal symptoms.

When someone is addicted to alcohol, either physically or psychologically, he or she will do virtually anything to get a drink.

Becoming an Alcoholic

Alcoholism does not occur suddenly. An alcoholic usually starts as a social drinker. A social drinker is a person who enjoys an occasional drink. He or she does not drink very frequently or for the purpose of getting drunk. However, as the person uses more and more alcohol, the disease takes hold of him or her.

People who drink heavily are usually not bad or greedy. Instead, they turn to alcohol because of an emotional problem. For example, some parents may feel very lonely after a divorce. Or a parent may lose his or her job. He or she may start to feel inadequate and lack self-confidence. Other parents are unhappy with their lives for some reason.

Alcoholics are not bad or wrong. They are people who are trying to find a way to cope with their problems. If your parent is an alcoholic, it is important to recognize that he or she has a problem, and that his or her drinking is not your fault.

The Disease's Effects

Alcoholism progresses in four stages. The first of these, the warning stage, is when someone just begins to feel the addiction. The alcoholic begins to look for reasons to get drunk more often, and will make anything an excuse to have a drink. His tolerance rises as his body becomes used to having alcohol in it. He goes from an occasional drink to drinking daily.

In the next stage, the danger stage, the alcoholic becomes drunk more often. He may begin to experience blackouts, periods of time he does not remember. He drinks alone, sneaks drinks, gulps drinks and feels guilty about his drinking but doesn't stop. He begins to miss work because of his drinking.

In the third stage, or the losing-control stage, the alcoholic starts to blame others for his problem. He withdraws and becomes unpredictable. He loses all sense of responsibility. He avoids family and friends, and sometimes has to be hospitalized because of alcohol.

The final stage is the loss-of-control stage. The alcoholic will accept any kind of drug, not just alcohol. He no longer makes excuses for his behavior, and his only comfort comes from a bottle. He shakes if he doesn't have a drink every few minutes. He can't do anything right. Often, the alcoholic develops all kinds of other diseases that are side effects of alcohol abuse, such as cirrhosis of the liver, high blood pressure, heart damage, and brain damage.

There is no fifth stage because, if the progress of alcoholism is not stopped, it results in death.

Who Becomes an Alcoholic?
Two-thirds of all adults in the United States drink

alcohol. However, 10 percent of these drinkers are responsible for about half of the total amount of alcohol consumed in the country. Thus, a very small number of people are drinking a very large percentage of the alcohol that is drunk each year.

You may wonder, if my mom or dad is an alcoholic, does this mean that I will become one, too? Scientists know that the children of alcoholics do not necessarily become alcoholics themselves. But they are at a higher risk for alcoholism than people who did not have an alcoholic parent. However, even people who do not have a history of alcoholism in their families can become alcoholics. It can happen to anyone.

Researchers have several ideas about why someone becomes an alcoholic. First, experts believe that genes put people at a higher risk. Each of your parents passes on genes to you. Just as a parent may have given you blue eyes or brown hair, he or she could also have given you a gene that puts you at a higher risk for alcoholism.

People who grow up in an alcoholic family may also learn to repeat the behavior that they see. If they see their parent using alcohol to cope with a problem, these children may be likely to do the same thing.

Other important clues to alcoholism are peer pressure and the availability to alcohol. If you feel pressure from friends and classmates to drink—and you have access to alcohol—your risk for alcoholism may go up. Also, the earlier you begin to drink, the higher your risk becomes. People who begin drinking alcohol before the age of fifteen are four times more likely to become alcoholics than those who start drinking at age twenty-one.

Who Can Help an Alcoholic?

There are several ways that alcoholics can get help for their drinking problem. All methods of treatment include completely quitting drinking. An alcoholic can never drink again—not even one drink. Once someone has the disease, he or she has it for life. Because there is no cure for alcoholism, alcoholics who have stopped drinking are called recovering alcoholics.

It may be difficult for alcoholics to seek help. Doing so means that they must admit they have a problem with alcohol. An alcoholic may be very ashamed of his or her behavior and want to keep it a secret. If your parent won't admit that he or she has a problem, you may want to find someone who can help convince him or her. A close family member, trusted friend, religious leader, or another adult may be able to encourage your parent to seek treatment.

Types of available treatment include visits to Alcoholics Anonymous (AA), outpatient treatment, and, for the most severe cases, inpatient treatment. You will learn more about these methods later in this book. Your family doctor or a drug and alcohol counselor can recommend the most suitable type of treatment for your parent.

Not all alcoholics drink every day. Some drink a lot only on weekends or at parties.

Chapter 2

Warning Signs of Alcoholism

Alcoholism can take many forms. Some alcoholics only drink on the weekends. Some only drink beer. Some seem to drink all the time. There are ways of telling if your parent is an alcoholic. But each alcoholic is different. James's mother drinks during the day. She only drinks wine. Karen's father usually drinks on the weekends. But when he starts, he can't stop. Maybe your mom or dad is like Karen's or James's alcoholic parent.

If four or five of these clues are true for your parent, you have alcoholism in your family. Without help, the problem will become serious for every family member not only the one who drinks.

1) *Your parent drinks more now than he or she used to.* Karen remembers when she was younger that her father only drank late at night on the weekends. Now, he starts drinking after work on Friday and doesn't stop until Monday morning. During the week, he usually doesn't do any drinking at all.

2) *Your parent's drunken behavior is very different from his or her sober behavior.* When James's mother drinks, she is sloppy. Sometimes she slurs her words and laughs out loud to herself. She gets mad more often, and sometimes even tries to hit James. When she is sober, she seems nervous, quiet, and more helpless.

3) *Your parent denies saying or doing things that you saw when he or she was drunk.* Karen always gets in trouble when she goes out on the weekends. Even though her father gives her permission, he always yells when she gets home. He says he doesn't remember telling her she could leave. Karen cries and runs to her room.

4) *Your parent lies about how much he or she has had to drink.* When James's father gets home, he yells at his wife for drinking all day. James's mother swears that she's only had one glass of wine and complains that no one trusts her.

5) *Your parent makes excuses for needing a drink.* Whenever anyone mentions his drinking, Karen's father gets very angry. He yells about how hard he

works all week and how much his family doesn't appreciate him. He says he needs to relax on the weekends. He says he takes orders on the job, but doesn't want to be nagged in his own home.

6) *Your parent likes to drink before he or she goes out to parties.* James's mother likes to be ready an hour before she goes out for the evening. She always has three or four glasses of wine at home. She tells James that she likes to be in "the right mood" when she gets to parties.

7) *Your parent hides bottles of alcohol all over the house.* Karen finds bottles of whiskey behind the swing on the porch. Her father goes out to the porch when Karen's mom goes to bed. Sometimes

For an alcoholic whose hands shake, threading a needle can become a difficult task.

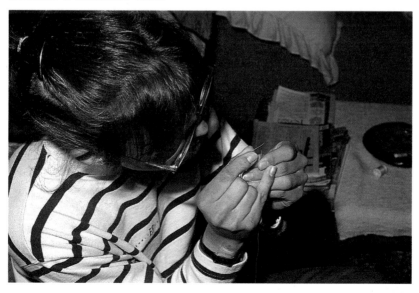

he falls asleep outside. Karen's mother cries when she finds him there in the morning.

8) *Your parent sometimes apologizes for things he or she did while drunk, and promises never to drink again.* James's mother tells him how sorry she is for missing his all-star baseball game. When James gets home, his mother cries and promises not to drink in the afternoon anymore.

9) *Your parent spends more and more time with friends who also drink.* Karen and her father used to play basketball on Saturday afternoons. These days, Karen's father spends his weekends sitting in the living room watching TV with his friends. They drink all day and are very loud.

10) *Your parent's hands are not as steady as they used to be.* James's mother used to knit and sew. Now she says she has no patience to do work like that. James sees his mother's hands shake when she makes dinner and does the dishes.

11) *Your parent often drinks instead of eating dinner.* Karen's father doesn't bother to sit down for dinner on the weekends. Sometimes he goes out to bars and doesn't get home until very late.

12) *Your parent doesn't keep promises.* James's mother makes appointments to meet with James's teachers at school, but never shows up. She promises James that she will go, but always says that she forgets. Each time there is a different excuse.

Alcoholic parents may try to hide their drinking by buying alcohol secretly or hiding it around the house.

What Is Happening to Me?

Another way to test your parent's drinking problem is to look at your own behavior and feelings. See what is happening to you. Read over the following list. If four or five of these statements are true of you, there probably is an alcoholic in your house:

1) I am ashamed to bring friends home because I don't know how my alcoholic parent will behave.

2) I am sometimes afraid when my alcoholic parent is driving the car.

3) I have a hard time doing my school work because I am worried about what is happening downstairs or in the other room.

4) I sometimes think that if I were a better student, or a better athlete, or more helpful at home, my parent wouldn't drink so much.

5) When my alcoholic parent starts drinking, I am afraid someone will get hurt.

6) I sometimes want to run away from home and not have to worry about what is going to happen next.

7) I have poured out all the liquor in the house even though I knew it would get me in trouble.

8) I don't like to admit to anyone—even my best friend—that my family has this problem.

9) I don't like holidays like Thanksgiving and Christmas. In my house they always end in my parent being drunk and ruining things.

10) I sometimes think my whole family is crazy and something must be wrong with me, too.

11) I hate arguments and don't ever want to hear another one.

12) I wonder if either of my parents loves me or cares how I feel. Maybe I am just a mistake they made and can't undo now.

Chapter 3

A Family Disease

There is no such thing as the perfect family. Every family has its problems. Healthy families deal with these problems. A happy family isn't happy all the time. The difference between a happy family and an unhappy, or *dysfunctional,* family is whether the needs of all the members are met. In a healthy family, even when there's fighting and unhappiness, these basic needs are filled. But in a dysfunctional family they are not. These basic needs include survival, safety and security, love, self-esteem, and growth. In an alcoholic family some or all of these needs are neglected.

Survival is being provided with food, water, shelter, and health care. In an alcoholic home, often these simple things are not provided. A child too young to care for himself can't make food when his parent is too drunk to cook. Survival is always threatened for members of an alcoholic home.

There is no such thing as safety and security for an alcoholic family. Alcoholics are often completely unpredictable, switching from mood to mood without any warning. Alcoholic families are always on edge, wondering what the alcoholic will do next. There is no sense of security.

An alcoholic can not provide love to his family. There is saying in AA: An alcoholic is having a love affair with a bottle. To an alcoholic nothing is as important as the next drink. Not even you. That's hard to hear, but it is the nature of the disease that an alcoholic cares for nothing more than alcohol.

Members of an alcoholic family have little chance to develop self-esteem. They don't feel loved by their alcoholic parent, and so they don't feel worthy of love. Often alcoholics are verbally abusive, telling their children that they are worthless so often that the children come to believe it. A child's self-esteem has little chance in an alcoholic home.

Growth may seem to be the one thing children of alcoholics do well. They are almost always more grown-up and responsible than other people. However, this is a false growth; they are shoved into more responsibility than they can

Healthy families talk to each other. Family members take part in activities such as family dinners.

handle and skip the process of growing up. They are made by the alcoholic parent into something they are not. They don't grow on their own.

Family Roles

In a dysfunctional family, especially an alcoholic one, every member takes on different behavior patterns.

• *The Enabler.* The enabler (also called a codependent) is usually the alcoholic's husband or wife. But the child of an alcoholic (often the eldest) can also be an enabler. The enabler cares for the alcoholic and takes on the duties that he or she is neglecting.

The enabler doesn't think about him- or herself but focuses all of his or her energy on the alcoholic. He or she does this in two ways. First, the enabler tries to take control of the alcoholic's addiction. He or she may do this by pouring out bottles of alcohol, lying to other people about the problem, or cleaning up the mess the alcoholic has left behind.

Also, the enabler often takes over the alcoholic's family responsibilities. He or she may do the cleaning, cooking, or laundry. The enabler will also care for the other family members when the alcoholic cannot. A child of an alcoholic parent often takes care of his or her siblings because a parent cannot.

The relationship between the enabler and the alcoholic is a complicated one. The enabler needs the alcoholic to function in day-to-day life. By focusing on the alcoholic, the enabler does not have to think about his or her own life, needs, and desires. He or she is coping with problems by putting them out of his or her mind.

Although the enabler tries to protect the alcoholic, he or she is making it easier for the alcoholic to drink. The alcoholism can then become worse. In this type of relationship, no one is truly happy or emotionally healthy.

• *The Hero.* The hero is the perfect kid. Usually the eldest, he is an overachiever, always doing everything right. He usually takes over the responsibilities of the alcoholic. Although heroes seem to have it all together, actually they worry all the time and are easily panicked. They feel that they somehow might have caused the alcoholism by not being good enough, and so are always trying to do even better. Heroes never feel good enough, no matter how well they do.

• *The Rebel or Scapegoat.* This is often the second child in the family. As the hero slot is already filled, this child decides not to compete, but instead to get attention by being bad. He does everything wrong, always gets into trouble, is completely irresponsible. Underneath the obvious anger the rebel feels hurt and pain. The rebel shows the bad feelings of the family, and at the same time takes attention away from the alcoholic by forcing the family to focus on his problems.

• *The Lost Child.* The lost child usually comes somewhere in the middle. When he was born, the family was too busy trying to cope with the alcoholism to give him all the attention he needed. He became withdrawn and quiet. The lost child tries to be invisible. He is terrified of anger and, in order to avoid any kind of conflict, simply pretends not to exist. He is usually very lonely,

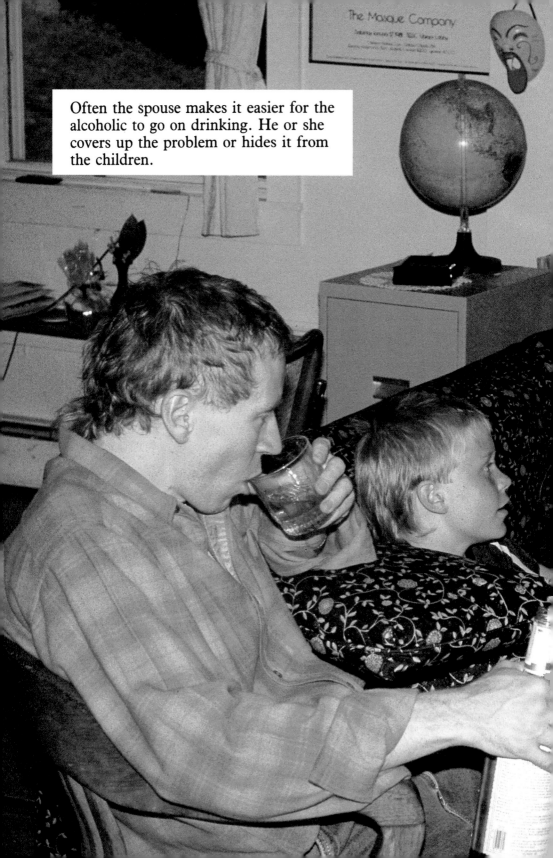

Often the spouse makes it easier for the alcoholic to go on drinking. He or she covers up the problem or hides it from the children.

and feels worthless because he gets so little attention from his family. He has never learned to relate to other people and has trouble making friends.

• *The Mascot.* This is usually the youngest child. He may seem spoilt, because he almost always gets his way. He is just so cute, the family says. He is a clown, always making jokes and jumping about. A mascot can't seem to sit still for five seconds. However, underneath the happy-go-lucky exterior of a mascot is fear. Usually a mascot has been protected from the alcoholism in the family by everyone else because he is "the baby"; he often has no idea what's going on. He knows something is wrong with the family, but the rest of the family tells him that everything is fine. He feels as if he's going crazy and becomes terrified of just about everything.

The reason everyone takes on these roles in an alcoholic home is that without these roles they would all have to deal with the pain of the alcoholism. *Denial* is very strong in an alcoholic family; no one wants to admit what's going on. Rather than talk about the alcoholism, everyone assumes these roles that allow them to function, but that also cause them pain. If an alcoholic gets help, you might think the family ought to be fine. That's not true. Everyone in the family needs help to learn to be themselves.

Chapter 4

Reaching Out for Help

You are not alone. Yours is not the only family with this terrible secret. It only seems that way. Most people don't know very much about alcoholism. Some people make fun of drunks. Others look down on them. No wonder so many alcoholics deny that anything is wrong.

You may be afraid to reach out for help. It is true that some people won't understand. But it is worth the risk. A friend or counselor can help you sort out your feelings and your choices.

A teacher, a minister, the family doctor, or a relative can give you practical help. Such a person can also give you the emotional support you need.

Look around. There must be an adult outside the family who cares about you. That person may

not know very much about alcoholism. But he or
she may be able to find someone who does. Or at
least that person can be a good listener. It helps to
talk through some of your practical decisions.

A friend your own age can like you without
judging your family. You should go places and do
things with friends. You need to get away from
home and have some fun. You also need to spend
time on your own hobbies and interests.

Support Groups And What They Can Do

Joining a support group is one of the easiest ways
to get help. Many other young people have the
same problem. Support groups are important in the
treatment of alcoholism.

At one time in the United States alcoholism was
not understood. Alcoholics were called "drunks."
They were often treated badly. People thought they
were weak and had no willpower. Being drunk in
public was considered a crime. Doctors treated
only the physical illnesses of alcoholics, such as
cirrhosis of the liver.

Doctors thought that stress, such as working too
hard, made people drink. They believed that if you
relieved the stress, the drinking would stop. When
it didn't, they said that the alcoholic wasn't trying.

That thinking was changed by two alcoholics. In
1935, a stockbroker and a doctor in Akron, Ohio,
got together and helped each other stop drinking.

Drinking keeps a person from using good judgment. This is why drinking and driving is a dangerous combination.

To stay sober, they met often. They talked about
their fight against their bad habit and about how it
made them feel. They had a friend who worked at
a local hospital. He was treating an alcoholic
patient. He appealed to his friends to help out on
the case.

The two men went to see the alcoholic. They
helped him to stop drinking. The frank talk and
support they had used with each other kept him
sober too. That is how Alcoholics Anonymous was
born. More than 50 years later this group still

Sometimes an alcoholic will become violent after drinking
too much.

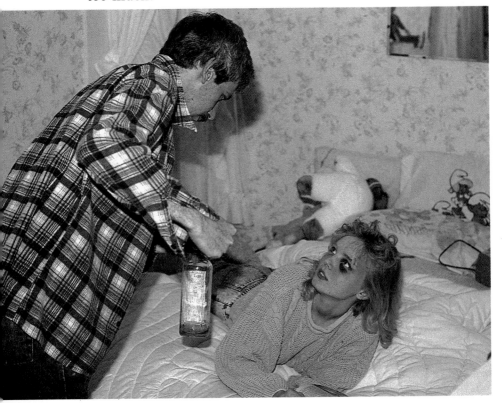

holds daily meetings. There are AA chapters in almost every community in the United States and in many foreign countries.

AA was the major source of help for alcoholics for many years. Doctors and social workers later became involved. In 1956 the medical profession finally recognized alcoholism as a disease.

Help for Families

Spouses of early members of Alcoholics Anonymous started Al-Anon. Al-Anon is a support group for the families of alcoholics. Its meetings are open to anyone who wants help.

Alateen, an AA-related group for the children of alcoholics, was founded in 1957. It was founded in California by the 17-year-old son of an alcoholic.

Most communities have an Alateen group. You can look it up in the telephone book. If there is no listing for Alateen, look for Al-Anon or Alcoholics Anonymous. Call either of those groups and ask for information about local Alateen meetings.

Alateen gatherings are very informal. They are often held in community centers or church rooms. Any young person can come. Meetings are free. Who you are doesn't matter. You don't even have to give your last name. You are welcome whether a parent is in AA or not.

Often an adult sponsor from AA gets the meeting started. But the discussion is among young people like you who have an alcoholic parent. You will hear some other teenagers tell their stories. They are going through what you are going through. Some of their experiences will be worse than yours. Some will not be so bad.

You may feel relieved to hear other stories. You may get some new ideas for dealing with your problems. You will certainly get help with taking charge of your own life.

You may be surprised to find that the talk is very lively. There is a lot of humor in support groups like Alateen. You may make some friends.

Alateen is not the only group for children of alcoholics. Ask around, or look in the Yellow Pages of your telephone book under "Alcohol Treatment Centers."

Talk to your high school guidance counselor. She or he may know of such a group nearby. If there are no local programs, your guidance counselor may be willing to start a rap session in your school.

Your parents may be glad to have you join one of these groups or they may not. They might think you shouldn't talk about family problems outside.

You are not being disloyal by joining a group that can help you. You all know that what you talk about is private.

If your parents can't see how the group is helping you, maybe a brother or sister will. Maybe they, too, can reach out for help.

Chapter 5

Coping With Emergencies

Alcoholics do not use good judgment. They can do dangerous and irresponsible things. They smash up the car. They fall asleep with a cigarette in their hand and start a fire. They stumble over furniture and fall. They often take other drugs when drinking. Drugs and alcohol together can cause death. Sometimes they beat up other members of the family. Sometimes they sexually abuse their spouse or their children.

These are ugly things to think about. But many children of alcoholics have to deal with them. They are less frightening if you know *ahead of time* what to do.

Drunk Driving

Driving while drunk (what the police call "Driving
While Intoxicated" or DWI) can cause trouble in
the family. Alcohol slows down the thinking
process and the body's responses. A drunk driver
endangers passengers and everyone else on the
road. Try to talk to your nonalcoholic parent about
this. Your alcoholic parent should not be allowed
to drive when he or she has been drinking.

You and your family must work out ways to
keep your alcoholic parent out of the car when
drunk. The other parent can refuse to go to a party
unless it is agreed that he or she will drive home.
You can certainly refuse to get in the car with a
drunk driver. Learn to use buses or subways.
Carry cab fare if you can afford it. Make sure you
have another way to get places you need to go.
Don't ride with someone who has been drinking.

Fire

Be sure you have the number of your fire
department handy at all times. Work out with all
the members of your family the best ways to escape
from your house or apartment. Have family fire
drills. Your fire department can help you plan the
best ways to stay safe.

Your house should have smoke detectors. The
batteries should be tested every six months or so.
Put yourself in charge of this important job.

Children should talk to the nonalcoholic parent about the problem.

Medical Emergencies

Talk to your family doctor about the fastest way to get help. Alcoholics often pass out from drinking. If they have mixed alcohol with other drugs—even medicines that a doctor has given them—they may go into a coma. Someone in a coma does not respond to anything. A person in a coma can die without ever waking up. Call for help as quickly as you can.

Alcoholics often have accidents. When they are drunk they are not very good at getting help. You may have to take charge. Be sure whoever treats your parent knows that he or she has been drinking. It can make an important difference in the treatment.

As alcoholism gets worse, scary things can happen. Alcoholics can have seizures. Convulsions or seizures are sudden fits. The victim falls down and loses control of her or his body. Arms and legs jerk wildly for several minutes. Then the person falls into a deep sleep. You should call a doctor. Loosen your parent's collar. Remove objects that he or she might hit and be hurt by. There isn't much else you can do.

Delirium tremens (DT's) can strike an advanced alcoholic. Someone with DT's shakes a lot and can't stop. This is as scary to the alcoholic as to others who see him or her. An alcoholic with DT's can have *hallucinations*. These are visions that are only in the person's mind. But they are very real to him or her. And they are often very scary. Call for medical help right away. There is nothing else you can do.

Physical Violence and Sexual Abuse

There may not be a way to stop an alcoholic from verbally abusing others. But we have laws to protect people from physical abuse. There are trained experts in every community who are ready to help.

If you are abused by an alcoholic parent, you can get help. Talk to an adult friend—a minister or rabbi, a teacher, a counselor, a doctor, a trusted relative. Ask where to go for help in your community. Or you can look in the telephone book. Check under "Child Abuse" in the white pages or "Human Services" in the Yellow Pages.

You may find only a drug abuse or alcohol abuse "hotline" number. These lines are answered by people trained to help in emergencies. The person who picks up your call may be able to tell you where to call or go for help.

If your alcoholic parent beats you, or your other parent, or a sister or brother, you can call the police. Go to a neighbor's house to use the telephone. Both your parents may be angry with you for doing this. They may feel that outside people should not be involved. They may think you have given away the family secret. You must use your judgment. Is the situation bad enough to risk their anger? Will they both seek help if they see how serious things are?

Get help if you are afraid that your alcoholic parent will hurt someone in the family. Talk with a trusted adult friend or relative about your fears. Don't wait until it happens again if you are scared. If your alcoholic parent hits you often, you need help. If your alcoholic parent tries to abuse you or a brother or sister, that is a good reason to ask for help.

Getting help is sometimes not easy. Ask an adult you trust to go with you. If the abuse is severe, you may be taken out of your home. That is a drastic step. But if things are very bad, it may be the only way to make them better.

No one deserves abuse. No one should be abused with words or with fists. No one should have to suffer sexual abuse. Every child deserves loving parents. If your family life is difficult, you will have to learn to accept it. What you *can* do is to make your *own* life different.

You can choose to take responsibility for yourself and your life. You can decide to help yourself. And you don't have to do it alone. Many support groups and social service agencies are willing to help you. You *can* take control of your own life. We will talk more about this in Chapter 8, "Looking at the Future."

Chapter 6

What You Can Do For Yourself

Alcoholic parents love their children as much as other parents do. That may be hard for you to believe. Your alcoholic parent may have said and done some terrible things to you in drunken rages.

Joanne's mother said that having a child like Joanne made her drink.

George's father told him that he was a stupid embarrassment to the family. He locked George out of the house for 24 hours.

Gracie's father told her she was a slut because she went to the movies with a boy in her class.

Louise's father accused her of forgetting to iron his shirts. Then he beat her for it.

What or Who Is at Fault?

How can these be actions of loving parents? The actions are not loving. They are cruel. But they are the actions of people with minds crazed by alcohol. The drug made these parents do what they did. The disease is more at fault than the parent.

Does that mean you should stand for such abuse? Absolutely not. Your parent should not be allowed to mistreat you.

If you are abused, you have a right to be angry. You should be angry. But try to focus your anger on the action and on the disease. Try not to be angry at your alcoholic parent. It is the drunkenness and the behavior that you hate, not your parent. It is hard to separate the two when you are being abused. Think about it later. It will help.

You may still have good moments with your alcoholic parent. If you do, you should cherish them. But that doesn't mean that you should put up with your parent's drunken behavior.

What You Can Do

You can gain more control over your own life. Separate your feelings about your parent from your feelings about the disease and what it makes your parent do. This process is called *detachment*.

A support group can help the family of an alcoholic to work out its problems.

You cannot make your parent stop drinking. That is a hard fact, but you must face it. Maybe you have tried. Maybe you have thrown out all the bottles in the liquor cabinet. Maybe you have even convinced your parent to promise to stop. You may be holding your breath, hoping it will work this time.

Your parent wants to keep the promise. Your parent probably loves you very much. But alcoholics lose control over their actions. They can't help it.

You can't make your parent stop drinking. That is a losing battle. But you *can* keep your parent from hurting you anymore. That is a fight worth putting your energy into.

You can help your alcoholic parent most by helping yourself. You can become a healthy person with a full, rich life. No parent could want more for a child.

Taking Control

How do you take control of your own life? First you separate your feelings about your parent from your feelings about what alcohol makes your parent do. Then begin to express your feelings.

If you love your parent, say so. You may hate things your parent does or says when drunk. If you do, say so when he or she is sober and able to listen. Talk to your nonalcoholic parent about all your feelings.

Break the rule of silence in your family. Having an alcoholic in the family can cause many problems. Look for quiet times to talk about the problems. Then talk about practical solutions.

You know, for example, that arguing with a drunk parent won't do any good. She or he won't remember it in the morning. You will be tired out and hurt. You will be frustrated. So don't do it.

When your drunk parent tries to start a fight, walk away from it. Take a stroll around the block if you can get away. Or walk into another room. Detach yourself emotionally from hurtful things your alcoholic parent says to you. He or she probably doesn't mean them.

Tell yourself, "That is the alcohol talking, and I don't need to hear it." If your parent insults you, remind yourself that the insult isn't true.

Don't let your alcoholic parent draw you into a fight with your other parent. You can say, "I love you both, but this is not my fight. You will have to settle it between yourselves."

Practical Solutions

Jerry couldn't study for exams. His parents' fighting kept him from doing his school work at home. He asked for permission to work at the library. He promised to be home by 9:30 each night. His parents were surprised at his request, but they agreed.

Maya felt frustrated, lonely, and scared. Her father had lost his job over a year ago and was depressed. He sat around the house all day drinking beer. When she came home from school, he yelled at her, called her names, and sometimes even pushed and slapped her.

Maya had tried to tell her mother what was happening. But she said that things were tough right now, and she was tired of Maya's complaining. Maya decided to take action. She asked an aunt if she could stay with her. Her aunt agreed to let Maya live with her until her father got help for his alcoholism.

Since his grandmother died, Hideki's mother was drinking even more than usual. She used to be in the PTA. And she used to go to all of his baseball games. But now she never came to anything at school. Even worse, she was always drunk when she left the house. Hideki was worried that someone they knew would notice.

Hideki thought that no one would understand—until he discovered Alateen. His best friend's mother told him about it and offered to take him to a meeting. Hideki said yes right away. He was so happy to know that he wasn't the only one with this problem.

Taking control of your life calls for hard choices. You know that you must be responsible for your own life. You know that there are things in your life that you can't change. But you don't always know what to do.

It helps to have somebody outside the family to talk to about all these things.

Chapter 7

Who Can Help Your Alcoholic Parent?

If you have an alcoholic parent, you may want desperately to help him or her. However, you cannot force anyone to seek treatment for alcoholism if he or she doesn't want to be helped. Because all treatments involve quitting alcohol, the alcoholic must be ready to commit to recovery. Although you cannot force an alcoholic to stop drinking and enter treatment, there are some things you can do to help.

You can help an alcoholic to see how damaging the drinking is to him- or herself, to you, and to other family members. If you want to urge an alcoholic to seek treatment, specialists recommend that you stop enabling, or trying to rescue, him or her. Lying, cleaning up, or covering up is not helping the situation. The alcoholic needs to face reality. He or she will be more likely to admit to the addiction and seek help if he or she is aware of the devastation that the alcoholism is causing.

Intervention

If you have stopped enabling your alcoholic parent, but he or she has not sought help, you may want to plan an intervention. In an intervention, you and others confront the alcoholic with the facts about the drinking. You tell him or her in a nonthreatening, nonaccusatory way that he or she has a drinking problem. You offer to support the alcoholic and ask that he or she gets treatment. Some tips for planning an intervention are:

1. Make your intervention with the guidance of a therapist, drug or alcohol counselor, or social worker. This person can lead the intervention and support you. Contact one of the organizations listed at the back of this book for information on interventions. They can help you find someone in your area who is professionally trained in making interventions.
2. Time the intervention carefully. Don't confront your alcoholic parent when he or she is drunk or angry. Wait until he or she is sober and calm, if possible. Be prepared for the alcoholic to deny his or her problem. Be persistent, but patient.
3. Tell the alcoholic that you care about him or her and want to help in any way that you can. Tell your parent you are worried about him or her, giving specific examples of his or her destructive behavior.
4. State how you plan to respond if your parent does not get help. This may be anything from saying that you will no longer make excuses for your parent to saying that you will move out of your home. Of course,

Cleaning up after the alcoholic is often an attempt to hide the problem.

remember not to make threats that you do not intend to act on, or ones that endanger you in any way.

5. Give your parent information about local Alcoholics Anonymous groups or other places that treat alcoholism. You may also offer to accompany him or her to meetings if you feel comfortable doing so, or find another adult that is willing to do so.

6. Get help for yourself from Al-Anon or Alateen. These groups provide support for the family members of alcoholics.

Individual, Group, and Family Therapy

If you've carried out a successful intervention, your parent will enter therapy. Maybe he or she even had decided to enter treatment on his or her own, and you didn't need to intervene. Your parent can choose several types of therapy. He or she may want to work one-on-one with a therapist, with a group of recovering alcoholics, or with the family members. Family therapy is usually necessary to work through the problems that alcoholism has created within the family. Often a combination of all three types of therapy works best.

The therapist or counselor helps the alcoholic to identify the problems that have led to alcohol abuse. The therapist will then help the alcoholic find new ways of coping with these problems. Counselors also often provide links with other types of assistance, such as education, job training, legal assistance, or parenting classes.

Getting an alcoholic to a treatment center is a good first step.

Outpatient Treatment

In outpatient treatment, the alcoholic lives at home but makes regular visits to a treatment center for therapy. At the center, he or she will be assisted by medical doctors, mental health workers, and drug and alcohol counselors. The individual, group, and family therapies that were described earlier are a crucial part of outpatient treatment.

Inpatient Treatment

In serious cases, when a person needs constant treatment, he or she is admitted to the treatment center as an inpatient. This often occurs because the person is seriously ill or in danger of hurting him- or herself. In inpatient treatment, the alcoholic lives at a hospital or treatment center for a period of time, often a month. There the alcoholic's health will be closely monitored, and he or she will receive psychological counseling.

To recover, alcoholics need to find new ways of coping with stress. Learning these skills is one part of the recovery process, or rehabilitation. Alcoholics are also strongly encouraged to join Alcoholics Anonymous, where they can receive encouragement and support. Recovering from alcoholism is a long, hard road. Many people have setbacks and relapses. It may be hard to see your parent working so hard to be sober and then slipping backward, but it is at these times that he or she most needs your encouragement. Remember, recovery takes time.

Chapter **8**

Looking at the Future

Everything you've learned in this book will help you to create your own life. That means separating yourself from your parent's disease. It also means taking control of your life.

You can succeed in whatever you do. One way to do that is to try to find the positive side of your experiences. Ask yourself what you have learned from the experience.

In living with an alcoholic parent, you may have learned many things. It may have been important for you to work on your self-esteem every day, for example. Or you may have learned that you were able to make tough decisions. You may have learned to be more independent and self-reliant than other kids. You learned about the dangers of alcohol abuse first-hand. You know how alcoholism can destroy a family.

Improving your own life doesn't mean you must forget your family. It means you must do all you can to understand them. By remembering your alcoholic parent's struggle with their disease, you may make better decisions about your own life. Get involved with support groups that will help you to understand fully how the disease of alcoholism works, and how each family member is affected.

Good counseling can help you to see things more clearly. It can teach you what your special needs are. It is a chance to talk about the kinds of relationships that will be healthy for you in the future.

Alcoholism does seem to run in families. You need to be aware of how dangerous it may be for you to drink, even a little. But be careful of making excuses for your behavior. There may be times when it seems easier to blame your family background for your own poor choices. You don't want to make the same mistakes that your alcoholic parent made.

Children of alcoholic parents may have to work harder to restore or maintain a positive self-image. But they can recover. They can take responsibility for their actions. They can set their own goals and work toward reaching them.

If you are a child of an alcoholic parent, take time to concentrate on yourself. You are a valuable person. When you build yourself a happy life, you will be able to share it with others.

It is important for children of an alcoholic to pursue their own interests.

Numbers You Should Know

Alcoholism and alcohol abuse is a very real problem.
If you are the child of an alcoholic parent, these U.S.
facts and figures prove that you are not alone.

- Alcohol contributes to 100,000 deaths each year.
  This makes it the third leading cause of pre-
  ventable mortality.
- More than 7 percent of people over the age of 18
  (almost 13.8 million Americans) have problems with
  drinking; 8.1 million are alcoholics.
- Sixty-four percent of high school seniors report
  that they have been drunk. More than 31 percent
  say that they have had five or more drinks in a row
  during the last two weeks.
- Approximately 43 percent of U.S. adults (76 million
  people) have been exposed to alcoholism in their
  immediate family.
- Nearly 25 percent of people admitted to hospitals
  have alcohol problems or are undiagnosed alcoholics seeking treatment for consequences of their
  drinking.
- Untreated alcoholics spend twice as much on health
  care as non-alcoholics.
- Each year 37 percent of rape cases, 15 percent of
  robberies, and 27 percent of aggravated assault
  cases involve alcohol use by the offender.

- Fetal alcohol syndrome, which is caused by a woman's drinking alcohol while pregnant, is the leading known cause of mental retardation in the Western world.
- Each year 4,000 to 12,000 babies are born with physical signs and intellectual disabilities associated with fetal alcohol syndrome.
- 3.2 million Americans (1.6 percent of the population over the age of 12) receive treatment for alcoholism or alcohol-related problems each year.
- Twenty percent of suicide victims are alcoholics.
- Heavy drinking is the single most important cause of illness and death from liver disease.
- Alcohol increases the risk of cancer. Two to 4 percent of all cancer cases are thought to be caused by alcohol.
- Alcohol can lead to inadequate functioning of the sexual organs, resulting in sexual problems and infertility.
- Heavy use of alcohol can lead people to act in ways that put them at risk for HIV, the virus that causes AIDS.
- Alcohol is associated with 47 to 65 percent of adult drownings.
- Up to 40 percent of industrial fatalities and 47 percent of industrial injuries are linked to alcohol.

Glossary

addict A person who is dependent on a drug and cannot control his or her use of it.

alcoholic A person who is addicted to alcohol. Also, someone who cannot stop drinking once he or she has started, whether it is every day or once every six months.

chemical dependence Need for a drug (alcohol or any other addictive substance) in order to prevent withdrawal symptoms.

codependent A person whose actions help someone continue his or her addiction.

dependent A person who is chemically dependent or psychologically dependent on a drug.

depression Feeling very low for a long period of time.

DTs (*delirium tremens*) Uncontrollable shaking brought on by drinking too much alcohol for too long a period of time.

dysfunctional family A family that functions in
unhealthy ways.

enabler Like a codependent, a person who assists
the addict with his or her dependency on a drug.

hallucinations Visions, sometimes terrible, of
people and events seen in the mind. They seem
very real to the person having them.

hereditary Passed from parents to children. Hair
color and eye color are examples of physical
hereditary traits.

intervention A process that helps alcoholics face
the results of their addiction. Family, friends, and
people from work are involved in bringing alcoholics to treatment.

psychological dependence To need a drug to deal
with stress or stressful emotions.

role model Someone who serves as an example for
others.

social drinker A person who can enjoy alcoholic
drinks on social occasions without becoming
addicted.

stress Mental or emotional pressure.

withdrawal symptoms Upsetting physical and
mental effects that alcoholics and other addicts
suffer when they give up the drug on which they
are physically dependent.

Where to Go for Help

Al-Anon/Alateen Family Group Headquarters, Inc.
1600 Corporate Landing Parkway
Virginia Beach, VA 23456
(800) 344-2666
(804) 563-1600
Web site: http://www.al-anon.org/

Alcoholics Anonymous (AA)
P.O. Box 459
Grand Central Station
New York, NY 10163
(212) 870-3400
Web site: http://www.alcoholics-anonymous.org

Children of Alcoholics Foundation
P.O. Box 4185
Grand Central Station
New York, NY 10163
(800) 488-3784

National Association for Children of Alcoholics
11426 Rockville Pike, Suite 100
Rockville, MD 20852
(301) 468-0985
(888) 554-2627

Web site: http://www.health.org/nacoa

National Clearinghouse for Alcohol and Drug Information

P.O. Box 2345
Rockville, MD 20847
(800) 729-6686
Web site: http://www.health.org

National Council on Alcoholism and Drug Dependence (NCADD)

12 West 21st Street
New York, NY 10010
(800) NCA-CALL
(212) 206-6770
Web site: http://www.ncadd.org

In Canada

Addictions Foundation of Manitoba

1031 Portage Avenue
Winnipeg, MB R3G 0R8
(204) 944-6200

Alcoholics Anonymous (AA)

Greater Toronto Area Intergroup
234 Eglinton Avenue East, Suite 202
Toronto, ON M4P 1K5
(416) 487-5591

For Further Reading

Coleman, Sally and Nancy Hull-Mast. *Our Best Days*. Center City, MN: Hazelden, 1990.

Coleman, William L. *What You Should Know About a Parent Who Drinks Too Much*. Minneapolis: Augsburg Fortress Publishers, 1992.

Jamiolkowski, Raymond. *Coping in a Dysfunctional Family*. Rev. ed. New York: The Rosen Publishing Group, 1998.

Taylor, Barbara. *Everything You Need to Know About Alcohol*. Rev. ed. New York: The Rosen Publishing Group, 1996.

Trapani, Margi. *Inside a Support Group: Help for Teenage Children of Alcoholics*. New York: The Rosen Publishing Group, 1997.

Yoder, Barbara. *The Recovery Resource Book*. New York: Fireside, 1990.

Index

A

addiction, 9–10
Al-Anon, 33, 50
Alateen, 33, 34, 50
alcohol as a drug, 11, 13, 42
alcoholic
  definition of, 6, 9–13
  help for, 13, 29, 50, 51
Alcoholics Anonymous (AA), 13, 22,
    50
alcoholism
  causes of, 11–13
  as a disease, 9, 10–11, 33
  effect on family, 20, 21–22, 24–25,
    28
  inherited tendency toward, 12, 54
  signs of, 15–18
  stages of, 10–11
  statistics about, 56–57
alcoholism counselors, 48, 50
alcohol treatment centers, 34, 52

B

behavior, learned, 12
blackouts, 11
brain damage, 11

C

children of alcoholics
  abuse of, 22, 39, 40, 42
  controlling their lives, 40, 42,
    44–45, 46, 53, 54
  roles of, 24–28
cirrhosis of the liver, 11, 30
codependent, 24
coma, 38
control, loss of, 11
convulsions, 38

D

delirium tremens (DTs), 38
denial, 28
dependence, 11
detachment, 42, 44, 53
driving drunk, 36
drugs and alcohol, 35, 38

E

emergencies, coping with, 35–40
enabling, 24–25, 47

F

families
  dysfunctional, 21–22
  help for, 33–34

G

guidance counselors, 34

H

hallucinations, 38
heart damage, 11

heredity, 12
hero, 25
high blood pressure, 11
hotlines, 39

I
intervention, 48–50

L
lost child, 25

M
mascot, 28
medical emergencies, 38–39

N
needs, basic, 21

R
rebel, 25
recovering alcoholics, 13, 50

rehabilitation, 52
responsibility, 11
   forced, 22–24
roles, family, 24–28

S
seizures, 38
self-esteem, 21, 22, 53, 54
sexual abuse, 35, 39–42
social drinker, 10
social workers, 33, 48
support groups, 13, 30, 43, 52, 54

T
tolerance, 11

V
violence, 39–40

W
withdrawal symptoms, 11

About the Author
Nancy Shuker is a freelance writer and editor based in New York. A former
editor at Time-Life Books and executive editor of several consumer and
business newsletters, she is also an adult child of an alcoholic parent.

About the Editor
Evan Stark is a well-known sociologist, educator, and therapist as well as a
popular lecturer on women's and children's health issues. Dr. Stark was the
Henry Rutgers Fellow at Rutgers University, an associate at the Institute for
Social and Policy Studies at Yale University, and a Fulbright Fellow at the
University of Essex. He is the author of many publications in the field of
family relations and is the father of four children.

Photo Credits
Photos by Stuart Rabinowitz.